KAT PERRINE

Cats

A Quick Guide to Fun Facts About our Feline Friends

If you can, help others; if you cannot do that, at

least do not harm them

Dalai Lama

Contents

1 Introduction

Throughout human history, the journey of the domesticated cat from wild feline to much-loved companion is a tale as mysterious and compelling as the creature itself. Thousands of years ago, in the middle of ancient civilizations and untamed landscapes, the wild ancestors of modern-day cats decided to edge closer to human settlements, drawn by the promise of easy prey in the form of rodents around grain and food stores. This decision was the beginning of a symbiotic relationship. Over the generations, these pioneers began to exhibit traits that endeared them to humans with their smaller size and more docile demeanor, as well as the unbelievable ability to communicate with those who gave them shelter and sustenance.

Throughout the centuries, these felines wove themselves into the fabric of human society, going from opportunistic hunters on the edges of human habitation to adored household members. While ancient Egypt elevated them to near deities, medieval Europe battled over their affiliation with witchcraft, and now, our modern world celebrates them as symbols of grace, mystery, and companionship. The evolution of cats, Felis Catus, happened over many millennia, tracing back to the deserts of the East, where their ancestors, the African wildcat, existed. This lineage, shaped by the harsh demands of a wild existence, laid the groundwork for the many behaviors we see in domestic cats today. Like the big cats, house cats are true carnivores. Even though they have been domesticated for thousands of years, they still have a solid predatory hunting instinct and use their stealth to stalk their prey, attacking with sharp teeth and claws. This heritage also ingrained our modern-day cats with their famous independence and territorial instincts, as well as their solitary streak and tendency to hunt alone. The act of marking their territory with scent, be it a cheek rub or more overt methods, echoes the territorial claims that were vital to the survival of their ancestors.

Modern cat behavior is woven into their evolutionary history. A blend of ancient instincts and adaptability has allowed them to transition from wild desert hunters to loved members of our households. They are a beautiful combination of affection, aloofness, playfulness, and predatory skill. They are loyal, loving, and often comical companions.

2 The History of Cats

It has been between ten and twelve thousand years since cats began their relationship with humans in what has been coined by an

Egyptologist, James Henry Breasted, as the fertile crescent in the Middle East. Also referred to as the cradle of civilization, its location is in the ancient Middle East, which today encompasses Iraq, Syria, Jordan, Palestine, Lebanon, Israel, Egypt, and parts of Iran and Turkey. Irrigation and agriculture grew here because of the abundant water and the fertile soil surrounding the rivers, the Nile, the Tigris, and the Euphrates.

With agriculture, the subsequent storage of grain and food, and the inevitable refuse stemming from these early civilizations, rats became a severe problem. The abundance of food available is why these wildcats became drawn to human settlements, food scraps, and the abundant prey in the areas. It was the beginning of their domestication, transforming them from solitary hunters into curious companions of humankind.

In Ancient Egypt, cats were elevated from earthly hunters to divine symbols. Egyptians began worshiping them as manifestations of the goddess Bastet, who embodied fertility, protection, and grace. This reverence for cats made it a heinous crime to harm one. Even accidentally killing a cat meant the death penalty. When cats died, they were mummified along with their human counterparts. Egyptians put cat images on their temples and tombs to guard the secrets of the afterlife and the realms beyond.

In Europe, however, cats went through a dark period when they were associated with witchcraft and superstitions throughout the Middle Ages; they faced persecution only to be valued again eventually as protectors from vermin and disease.

In Norse mythology, the goddess Freya rode a chariot drawn by powerful cats. In Japan, the Maneki-Neko has stood for centuries as a symbol of prosperity and good fortune.

Knowing what great hunters cats are, they became very welcome on ships to control the fast-breeding rat populations and prevent them from eating the grain and food stores, chewing into the sails, ropes, and even the calloused skin of the feet of sleeping crew members. Sailing with humans is how our feline friends came to travel the world and spread throughout different cultures and societies. It is quite the journey, and I only touched the tip of an iceberg.

3 The Secret Lives of Cats

E ven in sleep, cats remain sentinels. Their ears twitch at the slightest sound, and they are always ready to spring into action.

Cats wake from their naps prepared to play "hunt," explore the world outside their windows and screen doors, chatter at the birds and squirrels they cannot reach, play with housemates and toys, groom themselves, follow their people around the house, watching what they do with curiosity and great adoration, greet you at doorways when you enter, keep any sneaky insects, rodents, or even little scorpions at bay, or just dashing about on brief wild romps throughout the home to expend their pent up energy. They are busy, curious creatures!

The size range or territory of an outdoor cat can be up to 30 city blocks, and because they hunt small prey, they tend to be solitary hunters and have plenty to eat. If the food resources are plentiful, they may live in small groups of two to twenty-five, primarily females.

Indoor cats pick their favorite spots and areas in the house. But make no mistake; to them, the entire house is their "domain." Some like to hide away, while others want to be up and out in the open. Some are very social creatures, and others are not so much if there are visitors.

They love to play and hunt toys while they play, knowing they aren't real. Cats are always practicing their hunting skills. Practicing their skills is a reason your goofy cat may occasionally come at you and go sideways with that hump in their back. They're practicing with their bad self. Cats and kittens learn these skills and keep themselves sharp by playing, which is great entertainment!

Routine and territory are essential in a cat's life. As said before, cats are creatures of habit and thrive when they can count on their human routines. That way, their routines are not interrupted. They are incredibly territorial and mark their territory with natural pheromones by rubbing their cheeks or bodies on their family members (humans and other household pets), favorite things, and the area around their environment. Marking their territory also makes them feel safer and more secure in their environment.

Things to keep in mind:

If cats are not socialized, they may be more fearful and timid, possibly showing aggression towards other cats.

If they live in a stressful or chaotic environment, they are prone to serious behavioral issues, such as spraying, scratching, and aggression.

The importance of routine and their environment severely impacts their behavior and well-being.

15

4 Cats of the World

A journey through the world of cat breeds reveals a mosaic of fur, personality, and history. Each breed has unique traits, telling a story of evolution, human preference, and natural selection.

1. **The American Shorthair** is the epitome of the versatile all American cat. They are known for their excellent health, friendly demeanor, and coats of many colors and patterns. American shorthairs are our laid-back companions in the cat world, happy to play or just lay in a sunbeam.

2. **The Scottish Fold** is recognized easily by its folded ears, which give it an owl-like appearance. Scottish Folds are cats of calm and elegance. They have a gentle

nature and a tendency to bond with their humans, making them good companions who enjoy cuddles.

3. **The Munchkin Cat** is like the dachshund of the cat kingdom. It is distinguishable by its short legs and long body, which result from a genetic mutation. Their short legs do not slow them down, though; they are as playful and energetic as they are adorable, darting around with surprising agility.

4. **Bengal cats** have a striking, wild appearance, with glittery coats resembling leopard coats. They are very active and playful, and their intelligence makes them challenging and rewarding companions.

5. **Aegean Cats** Hail from the Greek Islands. They are natural hunters and seafarers, often seen lounging about or fishing in the ports. They are robust, social, and affectionate, with gorgeous semi-long fur coats that reflect their island origins.

6. **Ragdolls,** with their plush fur coats and sapphire-blue eyes, are considered gentle giants in the cat world. They are distinguished not just by their striking appearance but also by their docile and affectionate natures. True to their name, they will go limp when picked up or held, showing their exceptional trust and affection for their human companions.

7. **Siamese Cats**, with their striking almond-shaped blue eyes and sleek bodies, are considered the world's aristocrats. They originate from Thailand, formerly Siam. They have a rich history and distinctive appearance with their color-point coats. More than visually stunning, they are known for their intelligence and vocal nature. They are not shy about expressing their needs and wants and are known for carrying on lengthy "conversations" with their human companions. Their voices are as distinctive as their personalities; they have a wide range of tones and volume to help communicate their complex thoughts and feelings. They are intensely social creatures capable of profound affection, comfort, and companionship. For this reason, they do not like to be left alone for long periods.

8. **Balinese Cats** are essentially Siamese cats with long, silky coats. They are talkative, with a soft, melodious voice, and form deep bonds with their families. Their striking blue eyes and graceful movements give them an air of aristocratic elegance.

9. **The Burmese Cat** is the social butterfly of the cat world. They are known for their deep golden eyes and outgoing nature. Their muscular build and sleek glossy coats, combined with a playful, affectionate nature, make them the life of any party.

A few of the more rare and exotic breeds of cats that exist but are not limited to:

1. **The Kurilian Bobtail** is rare, with only approximately one hundred in North America alone. While we create many breeds with human assistance and manipulation, the Kurilian Bobtail is an entirely natural breed with very short tails, and no two tails look the same.

2. **The Devon Rex** gets its name from its origin, Devonshire, in the United Kingdom. It has a unique appearance with large eyes, a short muzzle, prominent cheekbones, and big, low-set ears, giving it a characteristic "elfin" look.

3. **The Norwegian Forest Cat** is native to Norway. It is very family oriented and tends to bond with several people at once. It is well known for its playful, active, fun-loving spirit. It is friendly with other pets, docile, and intelligent. Quite rare, it is found mainly in Europe.

4. **Egyptian Maus.** There are only 6,700 registered Egyptian Maus with the CFA (Cat Fancier's Association), making them one of the world's rarest cat breeds. This medium-sized cat is highly active, playful, and energetic, with well-developed muscles. It is also the only domesticated breed of spotted cat.

5. **Tonkinese Cats** are also known for being extremely active and adaptable to other animals and humans. They have a more innocent personality, are attention-

seeking, and highly affectionate. They make great dog companions but could annoy more laid-back animals since they need to be around other creatures with the same activity level. They are a cross between a Siamese and Burmese; they are brilliant, vocal, and engaging.

Each breed brings its own flavor to the vast feline world and offers just a glimpse into cats' diverse beauty and complexity. Whether through the lens of history, the diversity of their colors, or their unique personalities, these breeds, and so many others, underscore the draw of cats as pets and companions.

5 Understanding Your Cat

We widely accept that we are close relatives to monkeys and apes because we are all primates. It might surprise you that we share many traits with our cat family. Cats have 90.2% of their DNA in common with humans, making them even closer to humans than dogs. A cat's brain has the same surface folding as our brains; it is ninety percent similar to ours. Their brains have roughly three hundred million neurons compared to humans' eighty-six billion neurons. That fact means their cognitive abilities are much like a toddler's. They are like jealous toddlers in a house with multiple cats, like mine.

As for personalities, cats will often mimic their owner's personality, such as extroversion, openness, and emotional stability. Or the opposite, depending on the owner's personality. And just like toddlers are notorious for mimicking what they see or hear, the monkey-see monkey-do saying also applies to cats. They learn by observing other animals or humans completing tasks. When it comes to their memories, research suggests that they have a similar long-term memory and the ability to remember things the way humans do, able to recall their memories on demand.

Like humans, cats can also develop mental health issues like anxiety or depression. A change to their routines, a traumatic event such as moving or the loss of a family member, or a change to their physical health can cause signs of depression and anxiety in a cat. They also can develop OCD (obsessive-compulsive disorder), doing things like sucking fabrics, chewing on inappropriate things, and excessive grooming.

As for their physical makeup, cats' eyes face forward on their heads like humans, instead of the sides like dogs' eyes, so their peripheral vision is not as good as a dog's but a bit more expansive than ours.

A cat's skeleton is a masterpiece of flexibility. It has more vertebrae in its spine than humans, giving it an incredible range of motion. Their muscles are powerful and lean. These muscles give cats their famous ability to nearly always land on their feet (called the "righting reflex") and their fluid, swift movements, with jumps that sometimes defy gravity.

Our feline friends have rapidly beating hearts and efficient lungs, which fuel their bursts of intense activity. Their cardiovascular system supports their stealth modes and sudden sprints, perfect for a predator relying on surprise and speed.

The most striking feature of cats is their eyes. Thanks to large pupils and a particular layer behind the retina that reflects light, they can see in near darkness, which was essential for the nocturnal hunter throughout the ages.

Their ears, too, are highly developed and swivel like satellites, able to detect the most minor sounds. These abilities protected their wild ancestors well.

Cats behave and communicate in ways as nuanced and sophisticated as any language or society. At the crux of their behavior are complex expressions, signals, and actions, each with their intent and meaning. They speak in rich purrs, meows, hisses, and chatters regarding vocalizations. Generally speaking, a meow can be a greeting, a demand, or a sign of distress; all come with varying lengths and tones to convey different messages. A purr is often a sign of contentment but can be nervousness or possibly pain in specific contexts. Hisses and growls are strong signs of discomfort, fear, and aggression; they will make their boundaries known.

A cat's body is an entire canvas of communication all by itself. A cat's tail movements can be indicative of their mood. A high-quivering tail signals happiness, while a puffed-up tail can suggest fear and aggression. The position of their ears and whiskers further define the dialogue, with forward-facing ears showing interest and laid-back ears showing fear or aggression.

In the feline world, the eyes are indeed the windows to the soul. Slow blinking is a way cats show trust and affection and is often called "kitty kisses." However, prolonged eye contact in the animal kingdom may be perceived as a threat or challenge.

Now, let's talk territory. Cats mark their territory to communicate status, familiar things, and beings. Establishing territory through facial rubbing, scratches, or leaving a more direct scent marker, such as urine, is common. Their scent messages create an invisible map, visible only to them and other cats. Mapping out territory was a vital function in the survival of their ancient ancestors in the wild.

In essence, cats communicate through various sounds, movements, and behaviors refined by nature to express emotions, needs, and desires. Understanding this complex language can deepen the bond between cats and their humans, bridging us with empathy and care.

6 Bush Dwellers, Tree Dwellers, and Beach Dwellers

I f you have ever seen episodes of Jackson Galaxy's "My Cat From Hell," you have undoubtedly heard of dwellers. Jackson calls it "the confident where" of a cat. Simply stated, a bush dweller likes to be on the ground, behind a plant, or in a dark corner somewhere. A tree dweller likes to be higher up off the ground, and the beach dweller loves to be on the ground and out in the open.

• **Bush Dwellers** may lurk in dark corners, under a table or bed, or behind something. It isn't that they're scared, as some may believe. As a "hunter," they are most likely waiting to pounce on some prey, be it a toy, another house pet, or your ankles. I have a tuxedo cat who loves to do this. He will try to nab one of my other cats or come out of nowhere, smack or bite someone's calf or ankle, and then run away as fast as he came. My brilliant but onery boy, he cracks me up. They are a never-ending source of amusement. If a cat is fearful and hiding, it does what Jackson Galaxy calls "**caving**." It will find tiny spaces to hide away as if it just wants to disappear. A new rescue cat will often do this until it is used to its new territory and family members. Cats must feel safe and secure and know they can trust you to thrive based on your characteristics, behavior, and examples.

- **Tree Dwellers** are cats that are more confident higher up off the ground. Tree dwelling within your home can be anywhere above the ground, though. On a table, the back of a couch, in a chair, your desk, and much higher sometimes. My three girls like to sleep on the sofa or the back of it, on the lower cat tree I bought for them, on the bed, or my lap. They prefer to be off the ground but not so much up higher. They love to be able to observe everything from their vantage points.

Please note: If they are up high, say to the back of your refrigerator to "**hide**" and stay up there; that is not tree-dwelling. That is fear or avoidance. If that is the case, you may need to take inventory of their situation. Are they being harassed by other pets in the house, the children, or is there another stressful situation for them in your home? You want to help them become confident enough to become that tree dweller or wherever they feel most comfortable.

- **Beach Dwellers** enjoy being out on the floor, with their paws firmly on the ground, but they are definitely "out there." These cats are always out in the open, getting tripped over, mainly when they spread out on the floor to rest or nap. They aren't bothered by foot traffic; they convey that we can go around because they're not moving. They seem incredibly confident of their surroundings.

- **In between,** Some cats exhibit the behavior of both tree and bush cats, or even all three. They adapt more readily, which speaks to their versatility.

My fur boy likes to sleep up pretty high most of the time. His favorite spot is the top of our tallest cat tree, but he will happily sleep on our beds or the couch occasionally. While his active hours are mostly bush and beach dweller time, his sleepy time means tree-dwelling for him.

7 Dietary and Health Essentials

ats are enigmas, and their dietary needs are as unique as their personalities. Cats are obligate (true) carnivores from desert dwelling ancestors, two factors influencing a cat's diet. Being an obligate carnivore means they take their nutrition from mostly animal-based proteins. They lack the metabolism for proper digestion of vegetable matter. Even though they may eat other things offered to them, especially animal products like eggs, cheese, or honey, they are not a natural part of their diet and are not consumed very often.

They require higher levels of protein than a dog of the same size. High-quality **Animal proteins** should dominate their meals. Cats also require **Taurine** is an essential amino acid found only in animal tissue. It supports their heart health, vision, and reproductive system. **Fats** offer energy and help to absorb vitamins. Omega's three and six fatty acids are essential for healthy skin and fur coats. **Vitamins and minerals** are necessary in small amounts for their various bodily functions. Vitamins A, E, and B-complex and minerals like calcium and phosphorus are vital.

Choosing to get them started on a feeding schedule is wise. It is not advised to leave a bowl of dry food down for them to eat twenty-four hours a day. Dry food is full of carbohydrates, sometimes as high as 35-50%. While some cats do okay with dry food, allowing them to graze from the food bowl whenever they wish can lead to weight problems for some cats. Sticking to high-quality, nutritionally complete food as the basis of their diets, be it dry food, wet food, or a combination, is essential. Overfeeding is a common issue, so be consistent with their feeding times and ensure the food is consistent with their current life stage (kitten, adult, or senior). You can start by checking the packaging recommendations on portions and then adjust according to their activity level and body condition. Cats naturally eat several small meals throughout the day; try to mimic this schedule if possible. Occasionally, cat treats are OK if they don't take up more than 5-10% of their caloric intake. Variety through different textures and flavors will help keep mealtime interesting for them.

Always have fresh water available. Cats are incredibly picky about the water they drink, and if your cat still doesn't drink much, you might try a cat water fountain. Although giving your cat wet food will also give it some hydration. I finally broke down and got my fur babies a couple of fountains, which they love.

Preventative healthcare plays a pivotal role in health and vitality. Regular vet visits, timely vaccinations, and awareness of common cat health issues form the bedrock of our whiskered companions' health and well-being. Annual checkups help keep track of your cat's needs, allowing for early detection and intervention for any potential issues. Like any of us, a cat's health needs will change. As they age, making bi-annual visits will make it easier to monitor any subtle changes more closely. The veterinarian can monitor everything from their dental health to weight management.

Vaccines are a defense against any unseen threats lurking both indoors and out. Core vaccines like rabies, parvo, feline calicivirus, feline pan leukemia, and others will dot their healthcare journey, along with occasional booster shots.

The key enemies in a cat's journey are dental disease, chronic kidney disease, obesity, and hyperthyroidism; each disease subtly hides until it has taken hold. Recognizing early signs like a change in appetite, weight, behavior, and litterbox habits can prompt timely actions on your part. External threats like fleas, ticks, and heartworms are also villains, but the vet can thwart these villains with regular treatments.

Play and exercise are paramount for a cat's mental and physical well-being. Play and exercise are vital for many reasons: weight management, muscle tone, mental stimulation, digestion health, and social interaction, bonding with humans through play. Stalking and chasing prey (or a laser pointer) helps to prepare their digestive systems for what's coming. Chasing and tiring out their prey in the wild alerted the brain and prepared the body for eating and digestion and recreating that hunting instinct in your home mimics that process. But it's not just about their physical health. Play is a recipe for a happy cat. It gives them and you a chance to season the day with excitement and a sprinkle of stress relief.

The essence of cat healthcare lies in vigilance, prevention, and love. Regular play and exercise, veterinarian visits, vaccinations, and an eye for the ordinary that will recognize something suddenly unordinary will keep the feline guardians ready.

The goal is for them to lead long, healthy, joyful lives. Understanding your cat's health and nutritional needs is about more than feeding them; it is a form of care that supports their well-being and vitality so they can thrive alongside us in mutual affection and companionship.

8 Feline Communication and Social Behavior

Cats, the puzzling poets of the animal kingdom, communicate with a sophisticated language composed of vocalizations, body language, and subtle cues not recognized by the untrained eye. Complex and nuanced, this language allows them to convey a broad spectrum of messages to human and feline counterparts.

For their human companions, they speak a combination of vocal cords and body language. A purr as deep and comforting as a storm signifies contentment or sometimes healing. A serene moment between a cat and a caretaker.

The meow, a versatile instrument in their orchestra of sounds, can convey a greeting, a demand, or a sign of distress, with the tone and pitch tailored for the message and the listener.

Their body can also communicate volumes. A tail flicking around in irritation, ears pinned back in fear, or that precious slow blink that whispers trust and affection. They will also convey affection with the soft brushes of their fur or gentle headbutts, known as "bunting," to express affection and claim their human as part of their tribe.

They may also bring you gifts, a toy, a leaf, a bug, a rodent, or a bird if they go outside to show their prowess and, as an act of sharing, an inclusion in their world.

Among their kind, cats use a more complex and subtle language. Scent plays a leading role, with them leaving "olfactory signatures" in their wake. I am talking about a blend of pheromones and scents that map out their territory, identity, and social status. Their tail becomes a flag of intent, up high with confidence, puffed up in fear or anger, or tucked under in submission. Vocalizations change for the feline crew, the hiss and spit being a clear marker of boundaries and warnings, while their high-pitched chirrup is a happy greeting or call.

The world of cats is made up of whispered dialogue and silent understandings, showcasing their intelligence and adaptability. Felines are generally solitary creatures but often choose to be "selectively social." They stroll through life with an air of independence, like explorers navigating their territory. Yet, even in their solitary wandering, they desire to connect, to share moments with chosen companions, be it fellow felines or humans. Their selective sociality comes from the desire to grace a spot with their presence, not out of a need but out of a desire for shared warmth. In their world, social interactions are a curated choice, not a necessity. Cats can spend hours in contented solitude chasing shadows or laying in a sliver of sunlight, but they will often seek company on their terms. It is in those moments they show their capacity for affection and companionship. They will curl up on a favorite lap, share playful antics with a fellow feline or human, and offer a gentle headbutt as a token of their affection.

Their selective sociality is a testament to their complex nature, an extraordinary balance between the wildness of their ancestors and the warmth of the bonds they choose to form. Cats remind us that it's not about the quantity of interactions but the quality, choosing moments of connection that enrich them and us, to be honest.

If you want to introduce a new cat into your home with a current resident cat already establishing its territory, you should handle this carefully, considering each cat involved. It is best for everyone involved to introduce your cats gradually and systematically through desensitizing and positive reinforcement.

Suggested steps:

- Keep them separate for a few days. A spare bedroom or bathroom would be perfect. Set the new cat up with water, a bed, a scratching post, and toys in their own space, free to explore.

- Introduce them by scent first. You can do this by using a dry washcloth or hand towel for each cat, rubbing it across their fur, and presenting it to the opposite cat to smell. Do not be surprised if they hiss; it is normal at this stage.

- Next, encourage interaction through the door by moving the new cat's food bowl close to the door inside. Your resident cat will hear and smell the new cat through the door. Give your other cat a few treats outside the door so they will associate this with good things.

- It's time to let the new cat roam around alone. Just put your resident cat in a room and allow it to get exercise and grow accustomed to the surroundings. Afterward, when the new cat is back in his room, you let your resident cat out so he can walk around and smell the new cat without seeing him. Doing so is another way to help them get used to each other's scent.

- After a few days, you can start opening the door a crack so they can see each other without getting their heads through. Be prepared for hissing or growling, and if they try swatting at each other, close the door. Continue to do this periodically, a couple of times a day.

- Depending on how it is going, you can move on to letting them out together; just monitor their interactions closely. Do not punish, yell at, or scold your current cat for hissing at the new cat; that is a normal reaction. Watch for the precursors to a fight: fur fluffing/puffing up, ears laying flat, batting at each other, spitting, or yowling. If they appear stressed or do any of these things, it is best to separate them for a few more days. If these behaviors start, you can distract them with a loud hand clap, a pillow thrown, or a toy and separate them immediately. Please do not yell at or get between them if they are fighting.

Returning to the beginning steps might be necessary before allowing them to interact again. Just keep them separated when you aren't at home until you are sure it is safe for them to be together alone.

9 The World Through Their Eyes

Cats live in a world full of sights, sounds, and smells they can detect and understand much better than we do. Their unique senses help them to see in almost total darkness, hear the tiniest noises, and smell things we can't even notice.

- **Sight:** A cat has a broader visual field than humans, two hundred compared to our one-eighty. Although a cat's precision pounces in the dark may make it seem like they have on a set of night vision goggles, they do need at least some light. Human night vision is iffy at best, but the dark is a cat's chance to shine, pun intended. The light enters through the cornea, which focuses on the retina that lines the back of the inside of the eye. A cat's large cornea and dome shape allow the eyes to bring in the maximum amount of photons, which is crucial to their night vision capabilities. The cat's pupils are a narrow slit shape in broad daylight but can expand 300 times in the dark, whereas human eyes can only expand about fifteen times larger in the dark. The back of a cat's eyes has a particular layer of tissue called the "tapetum lucidum" that reflects unabsorbed light back into their retinas, helping them see better in low light and making their eyes shine. That is why you see their eyes glow if a light is shining in their direction in the dark. They also possess better peripheral vision than we do. Yet, they don't see colors and details as sharply as we can. They have fewer photoreceptors in their retinas than humans, and what they can see at, say, twenty feet away, we can see at a hundred feet away. Since cats respond more to motion than details and colors, their reduced vision does not slow them down by any means.

- **Smell:** Unlike a cat's other senses, their sense of smell is already developed straight out of the womb, leading kittens to a first sip of their mother's milk and colostrum. The particular tissue in a cat's nose that detects smells has 200 million cells compared to a human's five million. Another special odor detector cats possess is called "Jacobson's Organ," located inside above the mouth. I read that its receptor cells connect to the part of the brain associated with social, sexual, and feeding behaviors. I did not know that. I did know that when this organ detects an exciting odor, it causes a cat to curl its upper lip and open its mouth a little. That action has a name, the "Flehman response." I find it highly amusing to see when they do that.

- **Sound:** Moving on to their pointy little ears, which are more like furry satellite dishes, they can rotate one hundred eighty degrees independently of each other. This ability helps them hone in on a sound origin quickly. Amazingly, they can pinpoint sounds around six-hundredths of a second (the blink of an eye, or faster?) from up to three feet away.

- **Touch:** Cats seriously depend on their whiskers. Whiskers are longer and thicker than cat hair, growing from follicles packed with blood vessels and nerves. It makes their whiskers as sensitive as our fingertips. It also compensates for their less-than-stellar closeup vision. Sensitive enough to feel subtle air movements of possible prey and help them navigate through and around obstacles, they can determine if they can fit in or through things quickly. Whiskers can detect minor environmental changes, including air pressure, current, wind direction, and temperature.

In nature, before cats endeared themselves and moved into our homes, they lived and hunted in the wild, just like their big cat cousins. Cats are good at survival in the wild but feel they are both predator and prey. Feeling threatened makes them most likely feel like somebody else's prey. They know their reaction could mean the difference between eating their dinner or becoming dinner for another. This survival instinct is alive in them today, and they act accordingly.

These senses make cats great at exploring and understanding their environment. They use their eyes, ears, noses, and whiskers to know everything around them, making them skilled hunters, navigators, and curious friends who love to explore.

10 Cat Mythology and Folklore

Some of the most fantastic folklore and stories about cats throughout history are incredible, given our current knowledge of the world and how it works.

One ancient legend is that cats are one of the animals God did not create during the world's creation. After God covered the world in flood and Noah set the ark to sail, it became overrun with rats eating into food and grain stores. Noah is said to have prayed for a miracle, and a pair of cats just sprang from the mouths of the lion and lioness on board the ark. These cats quickly took care of the population of rats, save the original two. When everyone could leave the ship for dry land, it was said these cats were allowed to walk ahead of the grand procession of all of Noah's animals. The legend explains that this is why cats are such proud creatures today.

When humans first found smaller cats in ancient Egypt, they were eventually elevated to divine creatures, making it punishable by death if a person killed a cat, even accidentally. They believed that the goddess could take the form of a cat. If a housecat died, the entire family would shave their eyebrows off and mourn their cat until their brows grew back.

Adorned and mummified cats, and even little mummified mice, have been found in tombs with their adorned humans. Their likeness adorned the tombs as well. Egyptians had the goddess Bastet, a cat mother, representing aspects of the cat, including sexuality, fertility, love, and life-giving.

There are many legends about people who could change into cats. Some stories tell of wizards, shamans, and magicians that had this power, but the "shapeshifter" would often be a woman and a witch. People believed them to be a witch's companion who aided in the spells and carried messages to the devil. They believed witches could shift to cat form whenever the moon was full. During the sixteenth and seventeenth-century witch trials in Europe, they would burn, hang, or drown these poor cats alongside their mistresses.

In America, folklore has them crossing paths with the supernatural. In different communities, they would be, and sometimes still are, believed to be harbingers of bad luck or guardians of evil spirits.

Moving from folklore to fairy tales, we find lovely stories from history, like "Chip, The Enchanted Cat" from Russia, where a mother cat and her kitten are humans under a fairy's curse. "The Cat Bride" is a fairytale of transformation in reverse, where a cat becomes a human bride for a kind and gentle man. And then there is a well-known fairy tale, "Puss-in-Boots," retold and renamed worldwide.

Beyond the visual arts, which cats have been a part of for centuries, they have also permeated our literature and pop culture. With literary works like "Old Possum's Book of Practical Cats" by T.S. Elliot, "Alice's Adventures in Wonderland" by Lewis Carroll, and children's books like

"The Cat in the Hat" by Dr. Suess, these feline characters have captured the fascination and imagination of readers for generations. Along with the many television shows and movies with memorable cat characters, they have become firmly cemented in pop culture.

Moving from folklore and fairytales are some of the better-known myths about cats throughout history. As I mentioned previously, there are beliefs that black cats are bad luck. Other beliefs you may have heard: They will take you (or your baby's breath) away and suffocate you while you sleep, that they are nocturnal, cannot be trained, have nine lives, always land on their feet, can see in complete darkness, hate water, are natural enemies of dogs, they don't need their teeth cleaned, that they're low maintenance, and the list goes on. There are so many other ridiculous examples, but I won't keep going in the interest of keeping this book the short guide to cat facts I intended. Trust that none of them are true.

In every culture, cats have had to weave themselves through our myths and legends as symbols of the mystical and divine. Every day, they remind us of their bond with humanity despite ourselves.

11 The Future of Feline Friendship

Modern technology and societal shifts have changed how we coexist with our feline companions. This digital age has brought a new cat care and companionship era that seamlessly integrates these beautiful creatures into our ever-evolving world.

With the invention of smart-home devices, we can now monitor, feed, communicate, and even play with our companions remotely. Automatic feeders ensure they are fed on schedule, while cameras and apps allow us to peek into their lives when we are not around. We can see what they are doing, we can feel reassured that they are safe, and we can communicate with them. There are videos, games, and even a couple of cat "songs" that you can play for them to interact with and/or enjoy. If you are interested, the names of the "songs" I speak of are "Rusty's Ballad" and "Padma's Love" by David Teie. Technology has also enabled humans to help feral cats with safer shelters, heating pads, and heated water bowls in the dangerous winter cold.

Advancements in veterinary medicine and online resources have significantly increased our accessibility to healthcare. Telemedicine consultations, access to a wealth of health information, and state-of-the-art treatments have helped improve our felines' well-being and longevity.

With online cat communities and cat culture so prevalent now, cat videos and memes abound. Social media has turned cats into literal global sensations, creating communities celebrating every purr, pounce, and jump. Humans have literally elevated them from house pets to cultural icons, binding cat lovers from everywhere in a digital embrace.

Cats have become ideal companions as society embraces more flexible lifestyles, including working remotely. They offer comfort without needing constant attention, and their independent nature aligns well with our busy, interconnected lives. Cats continue to walk alongside us in this world of innovation and traditions. The beat of a modern drum now accompanies their timeless grace and endearing quirks. As society and technology evolve, so does the rich, connected companionship we share with cats.

Conservation efforts for wild cousins of domestic cats aim to ensure these majestic creatures do not become historical footnotes. Conservationists are working together through a blend of modern science, community action, and international cooperation. Protecting and expanding the natural habitats of these big cats is at the forefront, with initiatives to create and link protected areas. This initiative will provide essential corridors for these predators to roam, hunt, and thrive.

They are taking severe anti-poaching measures with more vigorous enforcement of the laws and surveillance technology like camera traps and drones. These help guard against illegal hunting, defending these beautiful big cats from human threats.

Community engagement is helping to transform former adversaries into guardians. Education and sustainable programs have turned the tide in human-cat conflict, creating a more harmonious coexistence.

Scientists are using genetic studies to bolster the population, ensuring genetic diversity and breeding programs that can replenish the dwindling numbers in the wild.

International global awareness campaigns help raise awareness of these creatures and their plights, rallying much-needed support for their conservation efforts and funds.

Through these and other efforts, the roar of the lion, the leopard's stealth, and the tiger's majesty are vibrant living symbols of nature's untamed spirit, preserving them for future generations to witness and enjoy. May they always persevere.

12 Conclusion

Cats grace our lives with a quiet mystery, bridging the wildness of the jungle with the comfort of the cushion, bringing with their serene presence the spirit of their untamed ancestors. Cats teach us the value of patience when they wait with anticipation until they can give it the butt wiggle and playful pounce we love, the importance of curiosity when exploring their environment with fearless wonder, and the virtue of independence as they saunter through our open doors with their tails held high. And with every headbutt and purr, cats reveal a desire for companionship as deep as our own.

If you haven't heard of this before, the Hawaiian word "**kahu**" refers to someone with a pet instead of being called a pet owner. This word has a deep spiritual meaning, implying that a person and their pet connect spiritually and that you are entrusted with them and their safety. "**Kahu**" can be translated as protector, guardian, steward, beloved, and attendant. I loved this the first time I heard it and considered it an honor to be a kahu.

Our feline companions have journeyed with us from ancient civilizations to the digital screens of our modern-day life, tripping our imaginations and enchanting our souls. They are our muses and comforters, silent observers, and spirited adventurers; they invite us to pause and marvel at the everyday.

In the world of cats, every interaction is a dance of mutual respect and love, an opportunity for connection. They are invited to stay within our human sanctuaries, loved and cherished across time and culture, enriching our lives with their complex and beautiful presence.

Resources

Turner, D. C., & Bateson, P. (2014). *cat psychology tag · Gwern.net.* *Retrieved from https://gwern.net/doc/cat/psychology/index*

Napoli, D. J. (2013). Cats rule in ancient Egypt. *National Geographic Kids.* Retrieved from https://kids.nationalgeographic.com/pages/article/cats-rule-in-ancient-egypt#:~:text=Dogs%20were%20valued%20for%20their,them%20treats%20fit%20for%20royalty

History.com (Ed.). (2023, June 23). *Fertile Crescent.* History.com. Retrieved from https://www.history.com/topics/pre-history/fertile-crescent

Arnold, C. (2015, December 3). Surprising things you never knew about your cat. *National Geographic.* Retrieved from https://www.nationalgeographic.com/animals/article/151203-cats-animals-science-communication-pets.

Fowler, C. (updated 2024, January 19) 8 Ways People are Like Cats: Genetics, Traits, and More. Retrieved from https://www.catster.com/lifestyle/how-are-people-like-cats/#:~:text=Brains,surface%20folding%20as%20our%20brains

Mediati, J. Recognizing the Normal in Your Cat's Routine. Retrieved from https://www.northhillanimalhospital.com/recognizing-normal-cats-routine/#:~:text=Action%20and%20Interaction%20%E2%80%93%20Know%20your,in%20a%20brief%20wild%20romp

Top 10 Rarest Cats in the World | Al Arabiya English. Retrieved from https://english.alarabiya.net/variety/2021/09/06/Top-10-rarest-domestic-cat-breeds-in-the-world

Sandall, P. Ship's Cat   Sea History for Kids | National Maritime Historical Society. Retrieved from https://seahistory.org/sea-history-for-kids/ships-cat/#:~:text=Cats%20have%20been%20welcome%20aboard,the%20calloused%20skin%20on%20the

Arnold, C. (2024a, January 2). Here's how your cat experiences the world. *National Geographic.* Retrieved from https://www.nationalgeographic.com/animals/article/what-its-like-to-be-a-ca

Arnold, C. (2015, December 3). Surprising things you never knew about your cat. *National Geographic*. Retrieved from https://www.nationalgeographic.com/animals/article/151203-cats-animals-science-communication-pets.

Cat Senses, How Felines Perceive the World | PAWS Chicago. Retrieved from https://www.pawschicago.org/news-resources/all-about-cats/kitty-basics/cat-senses#:~:text=Whiskers%20are%20extensions%20of%20the,sensory%20cells%20at%20their%20roots

Galaxy, J (2014) Location: Cat Confidence " | Animalist. Retrieved from https://www.youtube.com/watch?v=GNaGNZ7bISU